Weird Meat-Eating Plants

PLANTS

Nathan Aaseng

Enslow Publishers, Inc.
40 Industrial Road
Box 398
Berkeley Heights, NJ 07922
USA

http://www.enslow.com

Original edition published as *Meat-Eating Plants* in 1996.

Library of Congress Cataloging-in-Publication Data

Aaseng, Nathan.
 Weird meat-eating plants / Nathan Aaseng.
    p. cm. — (Bizarre science)
 "Original edition published as Meat-Eating Plants in 1996."
 Summary: "Examines meat-eating plants, including the different types of carnivorous plants, how they trap their
prey, why these plants eat meat, and where they are found"—Provided by publisher.
 Includes bibliographical references and index.
 ISBN 978-0-7660-3672-7
 1. Carnivorous plants—Juvenile literature. I. Title. II. Series: Bizarre science.
 QK917.A2 2010
 583'.75—dc22
                            2010016602

Paperback ISBN 978-1-59845-223-5

Printed in the United States of America

102010 Lake Book Manufacturing, Inc., Melrose Park, IL

10 9 8 7 6 5 4 3 2 1

To Our Readers:
We have done our best to make sure all Internet addresses in this book were active and appropriate when we went to
press. However, the author and the publisher have no control over and assume no liability for the material available
on those Internet sites or on other Web sites they may link to. Any comments or suggestions can be sent by e-mail to
comments@enslow.com or to the address on the back cover.

Illustration Credits: age fotostock / Photolibrary, p. 1; © Barry Rice, pp. 15, 19, 23, 25, 33, 35; Courtesy Everett
Collection, p. 6; Eye of Science / Photo Researchers, Inc., p. 37; Flora Press / GAP Photos, p. 43; Gregory K.
Scott / Photo Researchers, Inc., p. 4; Courtesy of Noah Elhardt, pp. 8, 12, 16, 27; Oxford Scientific (OSF) /
Photolibrary, pp. 20, 41; Shutterstock.com, pp. 18, 30; Stewart McPherson / Redfern, pp. 28, 38; Sturgis
McKeever, Georgia Southern University, Bugwood.org, p. 36; U.S. Fish and Wildlife Service, p. 10.

Cover Illustration: age fotostock / Photolibrary (A common wasp trapped in a Venus's-flytrap).

CONTENTS

Green Monsters

More than a hundred years ago, a doctor reported a hideous event that he had seen on the island of Madagascar. He described a tribe sacrificing a girl to a flesh-eating tree. The deadly plant was ten feet (three meters) high. Its 12-foot-long (3.7-meter) leaves bristled with sharp spikes. According to the doctor, the plant snared the girl in its long, snakelike tendrils. Then the murderous leaves closed in on her and finished her off.[1]

Other reports of huge, deadly plants have surfaced over the years. A plant in Brazil was said to lure monkeys with bright flowers and sweet aromas. Then it crushed and consumed them. Sailors in the South Pacific were warned to avoid an island where the Death Flower grew. This plant was said to form a gorgeous cave so large that people could walk into it. If they did so, the overpowering aroma would put them to sleep. The plant would then devour its unconscious victims.[2]

The idea of such deadly plants continues to fascinate us. Science-fiction writers often tell tales of killer tomatoes and other lethal plants that stalk humans. One of the most popular of these tales has been *The Little Shop of Horrors,* which has been made into both a Broadway musical and a movie. In this story, a rare and valuable plant requires human blood in order to survive. As it grows ever larger, these demands grow ever more gruesome.

Any educated person now recognizes such wild reports as complete fantasies produced by overactive imaginations. While our planet holds a wondrous variety of plants, it does not contain *any* that feast on humans or even on monkeys.

The very notion of plants eating animals is bizarre; it seems backward. Plants are at the bottom of the food chain. They provide meals for animals. We think of meat eaters as deadly creatures equipped with sharp teeth, claws, brute strength, and speed. Plants do not fit that description. Although plants have

Stories have been told about killer plants eating humans, but they are not true. However, they remain popular tales to tell. This image shows a scene from the movie *The Little Shop of Horrors* released in 1986.

some defenses against predators, they are prey to even the gentlest creatures, such as baby rabbits, fat caterpillars, or tiny aphids. Plants do not have mouths or stomachs for digesting meals. How could they possibly eat animals?

Searching for Killer Plants

The idea of plants eating animals seemed so absurd that, for hundreds of years and into the early eighteenth century, plant experts discounted such talk. True, plants had developed some weapons that could hurt animals, such as the sharp thorns of the rose and the blackberry bush. Plants had poisons in their leaves and stems that could kill animals. Certain plants with sticky leaves were so adept at trapping small insects that people hung them in their houses as pest control. These were all believed to be the ways plants protected themselves from animals. After all, how could plants eat animals?

In the eighteenth century, English settlers in America found a plant they called a Venus's-flytrap. They watched this plant snap shut and squeeze insects. Could this plant be trapping and eating these insects? It was a subject of great debate among scientists. Some believed the plant actually was carnivorous, or meat eating. But many said no, and thought the trap was just another ingenious way for the plant to protect itself against pests.[3]

For many years, people had noticed pools of water inside the pitcher plants that grew in North America and the Pacific tropics. Some discovered dead insects floating in that liquid.

Near the end of the eighteenth century, an American botanist (a person who studies plants), William Bartram, grew curious about some features of these plants. He observed that certain downward-pointing hairs in the plant seemed to invite insects to the water, where they died. Again, that could be yet another example of a plant defending itself by killing off possible enemies.

In 1857, a researcher named Cohn examined one of the tiny sacs on an aquatic plant called a bladderwort. Most people who knew of these sacs thought that they served as buoys to keep the plant afloat. But when the researcher opened one up, he discovered a tiny dead fish. About twenty years later, researcher Mary Treat found that the sac was a trap that could engulf tiny water creatures in the blink of an eye.

Before these studies, many experts had thought that plants were doing the unexpected—devouring small animals. And evidence from these discoveries further confirmed that belief. By the late nineteenth century, the famous biologist Charles Darwin proved once and for all that plants did eat animals. He found that these plants produced enzymes, much like the digestive enzymes found in animals. Furthermore, his careful measurements showed that the plants were absorbing nutrients from the dead creatures. Darwin's experiments also showed that carnivorous plants that were fed an occasional meaty meal were a little healthier than those that were given no meat.

A Different Kind of Carnivore

Since Darwin's time, botanists have identified more than six hundred species of carnivorous plants. Insect-eating plants live in all parts of the world, in many types of climates from the arctic to the tropics. Most live in places with wet, spongy soil, called bogs. The wetlands and bogs along the Gulf Coast of the United States are teeming with carnivorous plants. As many as thirteen species have been found crowded together within a few acres. Carnivorous plants usually grow in soil that is thin or poor in nutrients. This is why they eat meat—to get the nutrients they need to survive.

Most of these plants are fairly small. There are no killer trees or human-eating plants for us to worry about. However, there are plants capable of devouring animals as large as rats, mice, lemurs, frogs, snakes, and small birds. Others dine on scorpions, spiders, grasshoppers, wasps, flies, ants, slugs, snails, baby fish, and tadpoles.

Even the smaller plant carnivores are no less fascinating for their size. Some of the smaller animals in our world must indeed tread carefully around meat-eating plants. Beware the killer grasses! *Molinia caerulea,* for example, is a grass that catches and

Meat-eating plants typically grow in wet, spongy soil, such as wetlands and bogs. These wetlands are part of the St. Marks National Wildlife Refuge in Florida.

eats insects for a brief time in its life. The grass has small traps on it that spring shut on small prey.

Beware the killer fungi! Fungi are in a different biological kingdom than plants, but some fungi attack from the ground just like plants. One fungus, called *Arthrobotrys obligiospora*, contains looped structures. The loop draws tight as tiny creatures, such as eelworms, crawl through it. The fungus then digests its victim. Another fungus, *Zoophagus insidians*, sets a trap for tiny animals called *rotatoria*. It sends out short branches for the rotatoria to feed on. As the rotatorium takes a bite, the tip of the branch swells, and the feeder is trapped.

Some small animals must even beware of killer seeds! Seeds of a plant known as *Capsella bursa-pastoris* use a very pleasant chemical aroma to attract mosquito larvae. When the larvae arrive, the seeds release a poison that kills them. The seeds then release an enzyme to digest the prey so that it can be absorbed.

Most carnivorous plants appear harmless. They do not have the intimidating presence of a tiger or a grizzly bear. They look innocent, peaceful, even inviting. The carnivorous plants are among the most beautiful in nature, with delicate flowers of yellow, purple, and white. Their leaves may be etched with designs of green, purple, red, and pink.

Hidden within this attractive beauty are deadly traps that make these plants as effective at capturing prey as the most feared animals. Some plants kill and consume thousands of mosquito larvae in their lifetime. Some have developed such foolproof trapping methods that they can collect hundreds of prey in a single day.

A British scientist once wandered across a killing field that clearly showed both the carnivorous plants' incredible beauty and their deadly menace to small creatures. A dense carpet of low-growing sundew plants spread for nearly two acres in a remote, spongy bog. Droplets of clear liquid like diamonds sparkled on each plant.

A huge cloud of migrating butterflies swarmed to the meadow for a rest before they continued their journey. They never left. The butterflies stuck to the little jeweled droplets and could not escape. As many as seven butterflies writhed in their death throes on a single plant. The scientist estimated that this sundew stand killed 6 million butterflies in a single afternoon![4]

A *Pinguicula*, or butterwort, traps small insects with its sticky leaves.

Flypaper Traps

The simplest way that plants snare their victims is the flypaper technique. This method is used by *Pinguicula*, or the butterworts, plants that you would hardly expect to be carnivorous. You could study the plants' structure carefully and not guess that they feed on tiny animals.

Butterworts

Butterworts thrive in most parts of the world north of the equator. They are the kind of plant that easily blends into the background. Their yellow-green leaves lie flat to the ground in a crowded circle pattern called a rosette. These leaves appear to be greasy rather than sticky. In fact, their name comes from the buttery feel of the leaves. Only the tiniest, lightest insects need fear getting trapped in this coating.

A tiny gnat flying through the air detects a sweet aroma. It locates the source of this attractive smell: a small butterwort.

The gnat lands on one of the leaves. Too late, the unlucky insect discovers that the aroma was a lure. Its legs are now stuck in the greasy substance. The gnat struggles to get free. As it does, the plant produces more of the greasy substance. Before long, the thrashing gnat is so coated with the substance that it suffocates and dies.

The butterwort then releases enzymes to digest the nutrients in the insect. The leaf curls slightly to form a shallow saucer, which keeps the enzymes from spilling out. This is especially important when rain washes over the plant. The butterwort also bathes the dead gnat in an antibiotic. This kills bacteria feeding on the prey that might spread and cause harm to the plant.

Butterworts are not fussy eaters. Few other carnivorous plants will consume plants as well as animals. The plant leaves will curl up and digest anything, including seeds and bits of plant material, that contains nitrogen, which is present in all living things.

Sundews

The *Drosera,* or sundews, are somewhat more lively flypaper killers. Rather than waiting for the prey to kill itself, the sundews work to make the job go faster.

More than a hundred species of sundews grow throughout the world, although most species occur in Australia.[1] They live in many types of climates. Like the butterworts, sundews often grow in shaded, low-lying areas with other plants. Their leaves cluster

This close-up photo of a butterwort leaf shows the sticky substance that coats its leaves helping it to trap insects.

low to the ground. Some grow less than an inch high, while other varieties can grow more than two feet (sixty centimeters) tall.[2]

Sundews are strikingly beautiful, especially when their crystal-clear beads of nectar, which look like morning dew, glisten in the sun. These beads rest on top of tentacles, which are thin, reddish, hairlike stalks that rise up from the sundew's flat leaves.

A butterfly fluttering over a field detects the sparkle and sweet nectar of a sundew and stops to take a sample. As soon as it lands,

Crystal-clear beads of nectar, which look like morning dew, sparkle on the sundew plant. But it is actually a very sticky substance called mucilage that traps insects like these unlucky dragonflies.

it finds that the nectar is combined with an extremely sticky substance called mucilage. The butterfly's legs get caught. It tries to pull away from the mucilage.

This struggle signals the sundew to kill the butterfly. The plant has a unique way of sorting out a meal from a piece of dust, dirt, or a raindrop. Although these things may be heavier than the insects that alight on it, the plant will not waste time and energy on them. Only when it feels movement will it prepare for the kill.

The sundew's glands send out more mucilage. As the butterfly tries to pull away, mucilage sticks on to its wing. Meanwhile, tentacles begin to arch toward the insect. The plant has no central nervous system to coordinate movement the way animals can, yet somehow each tentacle on the leaf gets the message to bend in the right direction toward the prey.

The butterfly starts to struggle. The harder it fights, the faster the tentacles move, and the more mucilage pours out of the leaf. Eventually, the sticky tentacles reach the butterfly and press it down into the mucilage. The butterfly drowns in the sticky fluid. The sundew then releases acids and enzymes to digest the victim.

Some sundews have tentacles that can curl over the prey within a minute. Others do not reach the insect for many hours. These tentacles do not aid in the kill, but they do aid digestion by holding the prey in the fluid. Some have leaves that fold around the prey for the same purpose. A few sundews have such powerful digestive systems that they can absorb a prey's nutrients in a matter of hours.[3]

When the sundew is finished with the prey, the tentacles relax their grip, and the undigested shell of the insect falls away. It may take a week or two before the tentacles straighten up to their original position. Each leaf can capture three or four meals before it loses its ability to fold in on prey. It then dies and is replaced by a new leaf.

Sundews can be deadly killers of insects. Many botanists commonly find the shells of six or more insects on a single leaf. One researcher reported finding a sundew that had more than a hundred insects in its sticky grip.[4]

The sundew plant's tentacles help trap the prey and also aid in the digestion of the insect.

Byblis only grow in Australia, and they can grow together to form a hedge. In this photo, the *Byblis* traps an insect.

Byblis

The *Byblis* are a much less common form of flypaper killer. These very beautiful purple-flowered plants grow in Australia. One species reaches a height of more than two feet (sixty centimeters) and can intertwine with other *Byblis* plants to form a woody hedge.[5] It has been reported that sometimes *Byblis* hedges capture and digest small lizards and frogs that try to eat the plants' insect prey.

Pitfall Traps

While slogging through a bog along Alabama's Gulf Coast or in Minnesota's northern wetlands, you might come across a field carpeted with *Sarracenia*, or pitcher plants. Row after row of these beautiful plants with their green and purple graceful, trumpet-shaped leaves and dangling yellow flowers spread before you.

What looks like a peaceful display of nature's delicate beauty is misleading. Once you know the fiendishly clever lengths these plants go to snare their victims, you can almost begin to hear that eerie music they play in scary movie scenes.

Pitcher plants have developed a more complex method of capturing meals than that of the flypaper trappers. Like the flypapers, they do not actively subdue their prey, but they present such a well-designed pitfall trap that the victim cannot resist walking straight to its death.

Sarracenia purpurea, or purple pitcher plant, is a beautiful plant that has a complex method of trapping its prey.

Pitcher plants are common in North America, especially in low-lying, damp, sandy areas. The pitchers are long leaves that rise from an underground stem called a rhizome. They form a hollow, vaselike tube that is usually narrow at the bottom and wider near the top—the open end of the pitcher. Part of the leaf forms a hood over the opening.

A pitcher plant is loaded with lures. Its bright, graceful leaves and sweet aroma entice insects. The hood provides shelter for insects and other small creatures who want to escape the rain. The undersurface of the hood contains nectar glands that produce a sugary treat that insects enjoy. Some pitcher plants lay a trail of nectar that starts at ground level and leads up to the mouth of the pitcher.

The Trap

Once the prey lands on the hood, the pitcher plant lures it farther into the pitcher. The plant provides an even greater store of sweet nectar down at the mouth. The hood and parts of the neck of the pitcher often lack color. These areas allow light to shine down into the pitcher, so that insects are not afraid to go into it. The insect may even sense the pool of liquid at the bottom of the pitcher and believe it is more nectar.

As the insect moves toward the mouth, it may slip on the smooth surface into a region lined with stiff hairs. These hairs provide poor footing.

A pitcher plant uses its hood to lure the insect farther down into its pitcher, where the sweetest nectar resides. But this is a trick: The nectar is where the insect drowns!

At this point, the insect may sense something is not quite right about this easy meal. It may stop eating for brief periods, perhaps trying to sense where the danger is coming from. It may sense that the hairs mean trouble. Some insects try to reach over the hairs to get at the rich pool of nectar on the other side, but the nectar is just out of reach so that the insect will have to stretch far, and possibly fall down into the pitcher.

After a time, a flying insect may try to get out while the getting is good, but the colorless hood lets in so much light that it appears to be an opening to the outside. The insect flies toward it, smashes into the hood, and falls down into the pitcher. Some kinds of pitchers are spotted with uncolored areas. These bright areas appear to be windows. The insect that tries to escape through these fake windows gets a rude surprise and may fall to the bottom.

A South American variety of pitcher plant traps prey in yet another way. Instead of a hood, it has a tiny platform at the opening of the pitcher. There is room on the platform for only one feeder. If two insects battle for a spot on the nectar-laden platform, one will likely fall off into the pitcher.

Some pitcher plants deaden their victim's senses with poisons. *Sarracenia flava*, for example, produces a substance that acts as a narcotic. As the insect laps up the nectar, it becomes less wary and less steady on its feet.

Whether it is drugged or not, once an insect starts walking among the hairs, its fate is sealed. All the hairs point downward into the pitcher. While the insect can move around the hairs as it walks into the pitcher, it finds its way blocked by these hairs when it tries to turn around.

Just past the hairs, the footing turns slippery again. This portion of the pitcher plant is smooth and waxy. Now the prey is trapped. The path back to the opening is blocked by hairs; the path ahead is impossibly slick. The creatures slip and fall into the pool of liquid at the bottom.

Here, the pitcher plant has one more way to prevent escape. Some pitchers contain toxins that stun the prey. Others have a

The *Sarracenia flava*, pictured here trapping an insect, produces a poison substance that helps trap insects.

wetting agent that soaks the wings of flying insects so they cannot fly out. The wetting agent also breaks the surface tension—the force that binds water molecules together and makes it possible for many insects to crawl on the surface of water. With the surface tension destroyed, the insects drown.

Meanwhile, enzymes trickle down the inside walls of the pitcher and collect in the bottom. Gradually, the plant digests the nutrients of the victim and absorbs them through special glands. After a time, the pool at the bottom may become filled with corpses of the plant's victims.

Pitcher plants most commonly eat ants, flies, and beetles. They will also capture and devour crickets, wasps, spiders, and even small toads.[1]

Cobra Lily

Perhaps the only carnivorous plant that truly looks deadly is a type of pitcher plant called *Darlingtonia,* the cobra lily. This plant grows in mountainous bogs in western Oregon and northern California. The cobra lily gets its name from a section of leaf, near the opening of the pitcher, that looks like the fangs or the forked tongue of a snake. With its straight stalk and rounded, spotted hood, it looks like a cobra poised to strike.

The fanglike part of the cobra lily serves as a deck to make landing even more convenient for flying insects. It is laced with nectar and hairs that lead the prey into the pitcher opening.

This photo shows how the cobra lily gets its name with its spotted hood and fang-shaped leaves that make it look like a cobra.

Nepenthes

The *Nepenthes,* found in tropical regions of Asia, such as Borneo and the Philippine Islands, are similar to *Sarracenia* pitchers. These plants have long leaves that taper to a point and then form pitchers. They grow like vines, creeping along the soil and up tree trunks. Stems of *Nepenthes* may grow longer than sixty-six feet (about twenty meters).[2] The plant bears two kinds of pitchers: smaller, trumpet-shaped ones in the upper part of the plant and large, wider vases on the lower end.

Small creatures feed on nectar near the opening of the pitcher. Their feet become coated with a loose wax that causes them to slide on the slippery surface and fall into the pitcher. There, they are digested in a mixture of rainwater and enzymes.

This *Nepenthes northiana* found in Malaysia trapped a rodent.

Giant Carnivorous Plants

Of all carnivorous plants, two species of *Nepenthes* come closest to the human-eating monsters of science fiction. The *Nepenthes rajah,* or King Monkey Cup, has gourdlike pitchers that may be fourteen inches (thirty-five centimeters) long and six inches (fifteen centimeters) in diameter. The pitchers of the *Nepenthes merrilliana,* found in the Philippines, may grow as large as ten inches (twenty-five centimeters) in diameter.[3]

These giant *Nepenthes* usually dine on cockroaches, centipedes, and scorpions as well as smaller insects. But they are large enough to kill bigger creatures that occasionally topple into the pitcher. Field mice, rats, small birds, and monkey-like animals called lemurs have been found dead in the bottoms of *Nepenthes.*

The Fork Traps

Genlisea is a carnivorous plant that lays a unique kind of one-way trap. This small tropical plant is found in waterlogged soil in South America, Africa, and the West Indies. The *Genlisea* sends spiraled, two-pronged forks into the ground. The forks are from one to six inches (2.5 to 15 centimeters) long.[4] A small slit runs from the base of the fork down each tine. Tiny creatures can enter the slit at any point along the fork. Once they do, they are unlikely to escape. Rings of hair force the creatures in only one direction—toward a digestive chamber.

Trigger Traps

Plants that use trigger traps to capture prey are perhaps the most fascinating of the carnivorous plants. Unlike the flypapers and pitchers, which lure prey to a lethal spot and digest them, trigger traps strike suddenly. Like the fierce predators of the animal world, they have something that works like a mouth to snap shut on their prey.

Venus's-flytrap

A trigger trap called *Dionaea,* or Venus's-flytrap, is found only along the coastal plains of North and South Carolina. It was unknown to most of the world until two hundred years ago. Today, because of its relatively large size and fascinating explosive action, it is probably the most famous of all carnivorous plants.

Dionaea, or Venus's-flytrap, have what are called trigger traps that have a quick, deadly strike.

This white-flowered plant usually contains a half dozen traps that may be as large as three inches (about eight centimeters) across.[1] The traps are leaves, divided into two lobes that look like a partially open clamshell. Spines line the edges of these lobes. Three trigger hairs are arranged in a triangular pattern inside the trap.

The inside of the trap is bright red. Along with the usual sugary nectar, the color helps to lure an insect close to the trigger hairs. As the insect feeds on the nectar, it brushes a trigger hair. This sends an electronic message to the rest of the leaf: Prepare for action!

The insect is now one touch away from doom. A few seconds later, it bumps another trigger hair. Instantly, water rushes out of the inner cells of the leaf. This causes the two lobes to snap together in a fraction of a second.

This quick action is hard on the plant. A trap can spring only three or four times before it turns black and falls off, so a Venus's-flytrap cannot afford to waste the effort. It has two ways of making sure that whatever triggers the trap is really worth eating. First, the nectar is placed far enough from the trigger hairs so that a small feeding insect will not reach them. Second, the trap will not shut unless two different hairs are touched or one hair is touched twice. This prevents the trap from closing on a piece of debris that might get blown into it.

The plant does not clamp completely shut at first. It closes just far enough for the spines to overlap, like iron bars on a jail cell.

A Venus's-flytrap will snap shut on its prey after more than one trigger hair has been touched or the same hair is touched twice.

Again, the plant does this so as not to waste effort on small prey. The spines hold larger insects in, while smaller insects can scoot out between them. If no insect remains in the trap, it reopens within twenty-four hours.

If a suitable prey remains, the trap closes tightly. The two lobes may squeeze together so hard that the outline of the prey can be seen through the leaf. This action crushes soft-bodied insects and seals the trap so that it turns into a digestive vat. The plant releases fluids that drown the prey so that the plant can digest the nutrients. It absorbs the nutrients, using a process that may take several days. Then it reopens, exposing the undigested remains, which fall off or blow away. The Venus's-flytrap is then ready for another victim.

Actually, the Venus's-flytrap would more properly be called a Venus's ant trap, since large ants are its primary food. But it eats whatever it catches, as long as the prey is the right size. This includes flies, spiders, snails, slugs, and tiny frogs. Venus's-flytraps have even been known to eat small shrimp when the ocean floods into their domain.

Bladderworts

The plants that are most deadly to tiny aquatic creatures are the *Utricularia,* or bladderworts. They use what some botanists call "the most intricate mechanism in the plant kingdom" to snatch unsuspecting prey out of the water faster than the eye can see.[2]

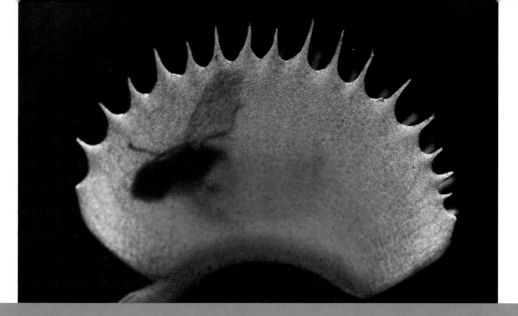

The outline of an insect can be seen through the leaf of this Venus's-flytrap. The two lobes of the leaf close so tightly that they can crush soft-bodied insects.

The nearly three hundred species of bladderworts are the most widespread of all plant carnivores, thriving from the arctic to the tropics. They are rootless plants that float free in shallow lakes, ponds, and quiet streams, or anchor themselves loosely in water-soaked ground.

The more common aquatic forms drift along the water, sending beautiful yellow or purple flowers above the surface. The business end of the plant lies below the surface. The bladderwort sends out a network of hairlike stems up to ten feet (three meters) in length. These stems are loaded with tiny balloonlike structures called bladders from which the plants get their name.

These bladders rarely grow as large as a quarter of an inch long—some may be no more than a hundredth of an inch. At one end of each bladder, there is a trapdoor that swings inward. Most of the time this door is sealed shut by a sticky substance.

The bladderwort sets the trap by pumping some of the water out of its bladder. This helps create a partial vacuum inside the bladder. You can get the same effect by squeezing the rubber tip of an eyedropper. As soon as you release the tip, it sucks in liquid. The bladderwort's door, however, blocks water from coming into the bladder. The pressure remains, so the bladder is ready to suck in water as soon as the door opens.

Along comes a tiny water creature, so small that you would need a magnifying glass to see it. The creature begins to feed on what appear to be strands of algae. In fact, these strands are trigger hairs that surround the door opening. When the creature touches one of these hairs, the trap springs with lightning speed.

The door flies open. The pressure created within the bladder causes water to be sucked in with such force that the entire plant jerks. The water sweeps the prey in with it. As soon as the water

Bladderworts float in the water and have bright flowers that show above the surface, like this one found in Bulloch County, Georgia.

This microscopic image shows the trapping mechanism of a bladderwort.

fills the bladder, the door closes. The entire process may take as little as one five-hundredth of a second. No creature on earth is fast enough to escape a trap that springs that quickly![3]

Bladderworts living in wet soil catch microscopic worms and insects that swim in the water below the soil. Aquatic plants usually gulp only tiny invertebrates (animals without backbones), such as water mites and mosquito larvae.

Because their openings are so small, it would be difficult to notice bladderwort kills even when their traps are snapping left and right. Occasionally, however, the force of the trap opening snares something larger, such as a newborn fish or a tadpole. Sometimes these unfortunate creatures are found with their heads stuck in bladderwort traps. A bladderwort can ingest one of these creatures by resetting the trap with the victim's head stuck inside, and respringing the trap to suck in more. The traps can be reset within fifteen to thirty minutes.[4]

Most carnivorous plants grow in soil that is poor in nutrients. The plants get nutrients lacking in the soil from the insects they trap and digest.

Endless Quest for Survival

Where did these meat-eating plants come from, and why do they attack animals? The answer is very simple: They need nutrients from the meat to survive.

Environment

Most carnivorous plants live in similar types of environments. In fact, many species often live side by side. They thrive in wet, sandy, high-acid soil. This soil is a poor source of materials such as nitrogen, phosphorus, calcium, and potassium—all of which plants need to survive.

If a plant had a way to get these elements from someplace other than the soil, it would have a great advantage over other plants in these areas. Carnivorous plants have done just that; they have gained an advantage in poor soil by capturing insects and other small creatures as their source of nutrients, such as nitrogen and minerals.

This advantage can be crucial. Carnivorous plants do not need to eat creatures in order to live and grow, but these plants are not likely to be as large or as healthy as actively trapping carnivorous plants.[1] A slight addition of nutrients to the diet is particularly important when nutrients are especially scarce. The advantage over other types of plants that carnivorous plants gain from their unusual feeding habits may be especially important during the tough times.

One such time could be during a long absence of fire. While we often think of wildfires as devastating, many carnivorous plants can survive them and even thrive afterward. Most carnivorous plants grow from hardy rhizomes that are buried in the ground. These are not affected by aboveground fires. In fact, a few botanists think that carnivorous plants need fires for their survival. Fires not only wipe out competing plants; they also release nutrients that have been soaked up by plants and return them to the soil.

Origin of Carnivorous Plants

How did carnivorous plants come up with their unusual survival strategy? How did they develop such amazing traps? Again, no one knows for sure.

One possible answer is that creature-trapping came about by accident. Many plants, not just carnivorous ones, are able to absorb nutrients through their leaves. Perhaps the original carnivorous plants had leaves that curled into shallow bowls. Water could have collected on these leaves in shallow pools that attracted insects. Some of these visitors could have accidentally drowned. The plants then absorbed nutrients from the dead insects, which gave them a survival advantage in areas with poor soil. Over millions of years, the plants could have developed leaves that were more and more helpful at capturing small creatures.[2]

New growth at the edge of a bog forest after a fire is shown in this photo. Some scientists believe that meat-eating plants need fires for their survival.

Giant People-Eating Plants

The slim survival margin that carnivorous plants gain from their activities helps answer questions about the size of these plants. People have long been fascinated with the idea of huge meat-eating plants capable of swallowing human beings. Could such creatures have existed, just as incredibly huge dinosaurs once roamed the earth?

No; nor would they ever be likely to exist. Meat eating provides a small advantage in gaining nutrients. The advantage is worth the energy that the plant has to expend to capture and digest very small creatures. A plant would need to use a huge amount of energy to capture and digest large animals. Bladderworts have great difficulty digesting the larger organisms that they catch. They may even die in the attempt. Venus's-flytraps turn black and die if they happen to catch a prey that is larger than what they normally can handle.

The fact that they have gained a competitive advantage does not mean that it is always easy for carnivorous plants to catch prey. Just as these plants have adapted ways to compete more efficiently, other creatures have adapted ways to beat these green carnivores' tricks. A wingless insect called a caspid, for example, has developed an antidote to the sticky glue of flypaper traps. It fearlessly walks up and down leaves that mean instant death to most other insects.

Hooded pitcher plants offer shade, warmth, humidity, shelter from rain, and a ready supply of food for any creature that

can avoid their deadly traps. Many insects have accepted the challenge of living dangerously. At least sixteen species of insects are found nowhere else but inside pitcher plants![3] Mosquito larvae and fly maggots wriggle among the blackened carcasses in the pitcher's pool. Coated with a special substance that helps protect them from the plant's digestive enzymes, they feed on the rotting and half-digested remains of trapped prey.

One species of moth spins a net across the opening of the pitcher plant to form a roofed home. Protected from rain and other insects, these moths chew on the walls of the pitcher. They have no trouble crawling up and down the walls that are so deadly to most other insects. Their special claws allow them to cling to the downward-pointing hairs. They walk down the plant backward so they do not have to try to turn themselves around when they are wedged in by the hairs.

One kind of spider avoids the slippery walls of the pitcher altogether by spinning a silken lifeline on which it drops down to the bottom of the pitcher to collect meals captured by the plant. Some birds have taken advantage of the pitchers' skill at capturing food. They slit plant walls with their beaks and devour the juicy corpses they find.

The most deadly enemies of carnivorous plants are humans. People do not see much value in the boggy areas in which carnivorous plants thrive. Because of this, the natural homes of the carnivorous plants are dwindling quickly. Every year, millions of acres of these wetlands are drained, plowed under, turned into pasture or farm ponds, covered by housing or industrial developments, or paved over.

Carnivorous plants have also suffered from their own beauty. Their bright flowers and the striking network of green, purple, red, and pink veins in their leaves have made them an attractive part of floral arrangements. Millions of plants are picked for bouquets every year. Until recent laws imposed stiff penalties on harvesting Venus's-flytraps, people picked these plants just for the novelty of having them.

Great care must be taken to ensure that the carnivorous plant species survive. Otherwise, the world could lose forever a fascinating group of plants—the curious little monster plants that have turned the tables on the animal world.

CHAPTER NOTES

Chapter 1. Green Monsters

1. Randall Schwartz, *Carnivorous Plants* (New York: Praeger, 1974), p. 118.
2. Ibid., pp. 122–123.
3. James Pietropaola, *Carnivorous Plants of the World* (Portland, Ore.: Timber Press, 1986), p. 15.
4. Michael Lipski, "Forget Hollywood: These Bloodthirsty Beauties Are for Real," *Smithsonian,* December 1992, p. 52.

Chapter 2. Flypaper Traps

1. James Pietropaola, *Carnivorous Plants of the World* (Portland, Ore.: Timber Press, 1986), p. 75.
2. Ibid., p. 76.
3. Randall Schwartz, *Carnivorous Plants* (New York: Praeger, 1974), p. 24.
4. Nancy J. Nielson, *Carnivorous Plants* (New York: Facts on File, 1992), p. 33.
5. Schwartz, p. 50.

Chapter 3. Pitfall Traps

1. James Pietropaola, *Carnivorous Plants of the World* (Portland, Ore.: Timber Press, 1986), p. 15.
2. Ibid., p. 40.
3. Ibid., p. 43.
4. Adrian Slack, *Carnivorous Plants* (Cambridge, Mass.: MIT Press, 1979), p. 116.

Chapter 4. Trigger Traps

1. "Adios," *New Yorker,* July 13, 1992, p. 26.
2. John E. Mathisen, "Plants That Eat Flies," *Minnesota Volunteer,* May–June 1980, p. 42.
3. Ibid.
4. Ibid.

Chapter 5. Endless Quest for Survival

1. Adrian Slack, *Carnivorous Plants* (Cambridge, Mass.: MIT Press, 1979), pp. 9–10.
2. Nancy J. Nielson, *Carnivorous Plants* (New York: Facts on File, 1992), p. 25.
3. Michael Lipski, "Forget Hollywood: These Bloodthirsty Beauties Are for Real," *Smithsonian,* December 1992, p. 52.

GLOSSARY

bladder—A flexible sac that stores liquid in a plant or animal.

bog—Soggy, waterlogged ground that is high in acid and low in nutrients.

botanist—A scientist who studies plants.

carnivorous—Meat eating.

caspid—A type of wingless fly.

enzymes—Proteins that perform or speed up chemical reactions.

fungi—Although they share characteristics with plants, fungi are classified in a different kingdom. Fungi include mushrooms, yeast, mold, and toadstools.

invertebrates—Animals without backbones.

kingdom—A classifying category of the highest rank, grouping together all forms of life that share certain characteristics. In biology, all living organisms are often divided into five kingdoms, three of which are animals, plants, and fungi.

lemur—A small, large-eyed, tree-climbing mammal, similar in appearance to a monkey.

lobe—A rounded division or section of a larger plant or body part.

mucilage—A sticky, gummy liquid produced by plants.

nectar—A sweet liquid produced by plants.

rhizome—An underground or underwater plant stem from which the roots and shoots of certain plants arise.

rosette—A circular pattern of leaves arising from a central spot.

rotatoria—Microscopic, three-sectioned roundworms.

surface tension—The binding force between individual water molecules that holds water together at its surface.

tentacle—A sensitive hair or stalk.

toxin—A poisonous substance.

FURTHER READING

Books

Halpern, Monica. *Venus Flytraps, Bladderworts, and Other Wild and Amazing Plants.* Washington, D.C.: National Geographic, 2006.

Johnson, Rebecca L. *Carnivorous Plants.* Minneapolis, Minn.: Lerner Publications, 2007.

Pascoe, Elaine. *Carnivorous Plants.* Farmington Hills, Mich.: Blackbirch Press, 2005.

Pike, Katy, and Paul McEvoy. *Plants That Bite Back.* Northborough, Mass.: Chelsea House Publishers, 2005.

Preszler, June. *Meat-Eating Plants and Other Extreme Plant Life.* Mankato, Minn.: Capstone Press, 2008.

Internet Addresses

The Carnivorous Plant FAQ: The International Carnivorous Plant Society
<http://www.sarracenia.com/faq.html>

Carnivorous Plants Online: Botanical Society of America
<http://www.botany.org/Carnivorous_Plants/>

Chomp! Meat-Eating Plants: National Geographic Kids
<http://kids.nationalgeographic.com/kids/stories/animalsnature/meat-eating-plants/>

INDEX